A Golden Age

ODYSSEY

Dedicated with love to the memory of Grandpa Carl Reutter, 1887-1982
—M.W.

To my daughter Meghan, with love and affection —D.B.

Copyright © 1996 Trudy Corporation, 353 Main Avenue, Norwalk, CT 06851, and the Smithsonian Institution, Washington, DC 20560

Soundprints is a division of Trudy Corporation, Norwalk, Connecticut.

Book design: Alleycat Design Inc. New York, NY

First Edition
10   9   8   7   6   5   4   3   2   1
Printed in Hong Kong

Library of Congress Cataloging-in-Publication Data

Wickham, Martha, 1963–
    A golden age : The Golden Age of radio / by Martha Wickham ; Illustrated by Dan Brown.
        p. cm.
    Summary: While on a field trip to the National Museum of American History, Emma imagines that she is her grandmother, sitting with her family listening to the radio as the end of World War II is announced.

    ISBN 1-56899-371-4 (hardcover), —ISBN 1-56899-372-2 (pbk.)
    [1. Radio—History—Fiction. 2. Family life—Fiction. 3. World-Fiction.]
I. Brown, Dan, 1949- Ill. II. Title.
PZ7. W6275GO   1996
[Fic]—dc20

                                96-15034
                                CIP
                                AC

A Golden Age

Written by Martha Wickham ❧ Illustrated by Dan Brown

Soundprints
Where Children Discover...

"Hurry guys! I want to see the Information Age Exhibit!" Emma calls. She and her friends, Lucy, Tomas, and Kevin, are at the National Museum of American History.

"I know you'll like this exhibit, Emma," Kevin teases. "It has radios in it." He knows that Emma always has her Walkman on.

Looking at the displays, Emma's friends all begin to talk at once.

"Wow! A telegraph machine!" notes Kevin.

"Look at the size of these old radios!" Tomas calls.

Emma begins reading aloud from a sign on the wall. It explains that the 1930's and 1940's were considered the Golden Age of Radio.

One old radio catches Emma's eye. "That looks just like the one my Grandma Emilia still has." she says. "She keeps it in her living room even though one of the knobs is cracked and it doesn't work anymore."

Her friends are moving quickly through the exhibit maze, but Emma is fascinated with the displays. Noticing some benches lined up in front of a video screen, she says, "You guys go ahead. I want to watch these clips from old TV shows. Let's meet back here."

The others agree and Emma sits down to watch. She watches the videotape three times and then decides to tune into her favorite radio station on her Walkman and wait for her friends.

Thinking of the old radio she passed earlier, Emma tries to picture her grandmother as a young girl. She wonders whether she enjoyed her radio as much as Emma enjoys her Walkman. Emma leans back against the wall and closes her eyes.

The music she hears is unexpected. Music with lots of trumpets and trombones and clarinets. Music that her radio station would never play! *This sounds like Big Band music,* Emma thinks, *the kind Grandma and Grandpa listen to on scratchy old records!*

Shifting her weight, Emma opens her eyes—and can't believe what she sees! She is sinking down into a cozy, overstuffed chair in someone's living room. A soft breeze carries the scent of spring flowers through an open window.

The music is coming from an old-fashioned radio, which is perched on top of a sturdy wooden table. Something about the radio looks strangely familiar. A family is clustered around it: an elderly man, a couple about her parents' age, and a girl a few years younger than she is.

They sure do dress funny, Emma thinks, looking at the girl's skirt and blouse. *I never wear skirts!* As she reaches to put her hand in her jeans pocket, she sees that she is dressed the same way. *Yikes!*

Emma doesn't think she's ever met these people, and yet she has the strangest sensation that she knows them . . . that she belongs here.

Emma's thoughts are interrupted by the mother's voice. "Emilia, sweetie, would you please go into the kitchen and get us all some lemonade and cookies?" Emma is startled to see the mother looking right at her! *Nobody calls me Emilia,* Emma thinks. *That's what they call my grandma—after whom I was named.*

Suddenly a strange thought enters Emma's head. No, it's impossible. She quickly looks back at the radio. *Could it be? Could I have become Grandma Emilia, back when she was my age?* Emma begins to speak, to ask what's going on.

"Shhh! Shhh!" the grandfather says urgently, turning up the radio. "There's an announcement!"

Emma notices that everyone is listening intently to the man on the radio. He sounds very excited. Emma tries to follow what he is saying, but understands only snatches. "It appears the Nazis are ready for a full surrender. . . . At this very moment, it is believed that they are negotiating a surrender in Northern Italy. . . . German troops are moving toward the Swedish frontier, ready to surrender to the Allies . . ."

It sounds like they're talking about World War II, Emma thinks, recognizing phrases from one of her schoolbooks. *I wish Lucy were here. She knows everything about history!*

Emma decides there's nothing she can do but go along with this and see what happens. She remembers that she's supposed to be getting lemonade. But which way is the kitchen? She decides to try the swinging door next to the dining room table, just like the one in her own house.

Luckily, she's guessed right. Pushing through the door, Emma finds herself in the kitchen, which looks nothing like her family's modern kitchen. There's a big white stove, with legs no less! The boxy, short refrigerator has no ice dispenser, or any colorful magnets on the door! And there's no dishwasher!

On the counter is a tray holding a frosty pitcher of lemonade and a plate piled high with cookies. Next to the cookies, Emma spots a newspaper, and she looks to see what the date is. The paper says Monday, May 7, 1945. Now Emma knows why the radio announcer was talking about World War II. She is pretty sure that was the year the war ended.

A familiar photograph on the shelf above the stove catches Emma's attention. It shows a handsome soldier in uniform. She suddenly realizes where she's seen the photograph—in her own mother's scrapbook. It's her Great-uncle Stewart, Grandma's older brother, as a young man. She's heard about his army days in Europe during World War II.

Emma peeks out into the living room at the rest of the family. *The girl must be Grandma's sister, Great-aunt Sarah. Those are their parents, Great-grandma Rose and Great-grandpa Carl. And that's my eccentric Great-great-grandpa Louis,* she figures. She's heard tons of stories about these people from her own Grandma, and now here they are, right in front of her!

15

Emma returns to the living room with the tray. As the family sips lemonade and crunches cookies, they turn the dials and listen to several different war updates on the radio. They look very tense, and Emma understands that hearing reports on the war must be very important to them. *How strange it is not to have a television!* Emma thinks. But the radio seems to be giving them all the news they need.

"I remember, as though it were yesterday, when this whole thing started," Grandpa notes. "Remember the awful news of the Japanese attacking Pearl Harbor?"

"Yes, I certainly do." Mother's face grows sad. "It was a Sunday morning. We'd just come in from church and turned on the radio when the announcement came."

"That certainly was a gloomy day," Father adds, "I knew it meant that Stewart would have to go and fight."

16

"Mother, if the war is ending, will Stewart be coming home soon?" Sarah asks.

"I hope so." Mother answers in a quiet voice.

"I'm sure he will be," Emma says firmly. She wishes she could tell them what she knows—that Great Uncle Stewart did come home safely from the war. After all, she was just at his house for dinner last week!

Sensing the anxiety in the room, Grandpa tries to cheer everyone up. "Son, do you recall another day when we were eager for news from the radio—back in 1927?"

"What happened then?" Emma pipes up.

"Grandpa's talking about the day Charlie Lindbergh flew all the way across the Atlantic Ocean," Father says. "He flew from New York to Paris in thirty-three and one half hours, all by himself, in a tiny little airplane."

"That was something!" Mother says.

"I remember when it used to take weeks to get news from around the world," Grandpa says. "Now, we just tune in to hear all kinds of things: the news, comedy, mysteries, quiz shows, soaps. Although my special favorite is still listening to dance music." He smiles to himself.

"You and Grandma were wonderful dancers," Mother says.

"Um . . . Mother," Emma says awkwardly. It feels funny to call someone else Mother. "What's your favorite radio show?"

"In the mid-thirties, I used to look forward to President Roosevelt's Fireside Chats," Mother says. "This whole country was deep in the Great Depression. Lots of people had lost their jobs and their money. Everyone was worried about what was happening. The President told us exactly how he'd save the country. It felt as though he were right here in this room."

"I've always liked Jack Benny," Father says. "He's so funny!"

"I like *The Shadow!*" Sarah chimes in.

"What about you, Emilia? What do you like most on the radio?" Mother asks. Emma pauses for a moment, unsure what to say. "I like listening to music," she answers at last. They'd sure be surprised if they heard the rock music she likes best!

"Speaking of favorite shows, it's time for my soap opera," Mother says, turning the dial on the radio. "I don't think there's any more news of the war for now." Emma notices that she still seems tense, and knows she's thinking of her son, so far away.

"Grandpa and I will be on the porch," Father says. "There's a ball game on."

As the two men leave the room, Mother brings in a basket of knitting. Music swells from the radio and the announcer introduces the next program. Emma is startled when she hears that it is *The Guiding Light.* Her own mother watches that show on television! Can it really have been playing for over fifty years? Then she realizes that the TV show must have been named for this radio show.

Sarah sits down on the floor and begins working on her homework. Emma helps Mother roll a ball of yarn. As she listens to the radio, Emma is pulled into the drama unfolding, and hangs on every word.

"I love you darling," a man's voice says.

"You know you're the only one for me," a woman replies.

Emma has fun imagining what each character looks like and what they might be wearing. She never realized that listening to the radio could be as interesting as watching television!

As the closing music for *The Guiding Light* fades away, a news bulletin comes over the radio. "Quick, call your father," Mother says.

Emma runs to get Father and Grandpa from the porch. The whole family stands in the living room, listening as the announcer says, "Tomorrow morning at precisely nine o'clock, President Truman will make an official announcement declaring Victory in Europe Day. I repeat, the war in Europe is over!"

Everyone starts shouting and hugging each other at once. Mother is crying and Father has tears in his eyes. "Well, it's about time," Grandpa says sternly, but Emma can see that he is smiling. Sarah is jumping up and down. Even Emma, who knows the war ended long ago, joins in, hugging the others excitedly. The family's joy and relief is infectious. They are almost delirious with happiness.

Just then there is a knock at the door.

"Come in," calls Mother.

The door swings open and a stout woman stands beaming in the doorway.

"Mrs. Austin, I guess you've heard the news, too," cries Mother.

"Isn't it fabulous?" Mrs. Austin says, hurrying into the room and giving them all big hugs. "Our sons will be home soon!"

After the excitement has died down a bit, Mother invites Mrs. Austin, her husband, and younger son to dinner. Mrs. Austin leaves to collect the rest of her family. When they return, the whole group feasts on pot roast, baked potatoes, and string beans. Emma feels right at home. This is the kind of meal her Grandma always prepares for her.

"I'm glad this war is nearly over, because I'm almost out of ration coupons!" Mother says.

Emma notices that Sarah and David Austin are constantly looking at the clock. It is almost nine o'clock. Finally, they beg to be excused from the table to go listen to their favorite show, *Lux Radio Theatre.*

"Let's all pitch in to clean up the supper things," Father suggests. "Then everyone can relax in the living room."

The children rush to clear the table, while the men wash the dishes and the women dry and put them away. In no time at all, the kitchen is spotless.

Emma joins the two families in the living room and sits down in the cozy armchair where she first found herself earlier that day. As *Lux Radio Theatre* begins, she again feels herself becoming engrossed in what is happening on the radio. She can't believe how powerful it is. She never imagined that a program on the radio could have you on the edge of your seat!

Emma looks at the people gathered around her. Their faces are cheerful and relaxed now, even in this tense and difficult time. She realizes just how important the radio is to them. They rely on it for current news from around the world, and for all kinds of entertainment.

Emma now understands why her grandma continues to keep her old radio in the living room, even though it doesn't work anymore. It was the center of so many wonderful memories from her childhood. *I'll have to ask her more about it next time I see her,* she thinks.

Emma curls up in the comfortable chair, tucking the long edges of her skirt around her feet. She sits back and closes her eyes.

*S*uddenly, Emma hears a burst of rock music. She opens her eyes and gasps with surprise. She is in the museum and Tomas, Lucy, and Kevin are standing in front of her. She turns down the volume on her Walkman.

"Emma! Hey, Emma!" Tomas's teasing voice sounds good to Emma's ears.

"Are you okay? You seemed fifty million miles away." Lucy's tone is light but concerned.

"No, just fifty years away!" Emma says under her breath. Out loud she says, "I'm fine. Hey, Lucy, when did World War II end?"

Lucy seems surprised by her question. "Victory in Europe, VE Day, was declared May 8, 1945. Victory over Japan, or VJ Day, was declared just a few months later, on August 14. Why do you ask?"

"No reason," Emma says, "just curious."

She smiles to herself as she pictures *her* family clustered around the radio, hearing the happy news at last!

About the Golden Age of Radio

The 1930's and early 1940's are called the Golden Age of Radio. Radios had become affordable for most families and, as television was not yet popularized, Americans began to rely on this new medium for both information and entertainment. The radio was the heart of the house and helped to soften the hard times of the Great Depression and World War II.

The radio provided almost instant information from across the country and around the world. Many people first learned about the Japanese attack on Pearl Harbor and the Allied victory by listening to their radios. Many heard President Roosevelt's comforting Fireside Chats, which he delivered to the nation during the Depression, and the famous words of baseball great, Lou Gehrig, dying of amyotrophic lateral sclerosis, at Yankee Stadium: "I consider myself to be the luckiest man on the face of the earth."

The radio offered something in entertainment for everyone. While doing the laundry, housewives passed the time with soap operas such as *The Guiding Light*. Men were able to listen to ball games and root for their favorite teams. In the evenings, families gathered for laughs with Jack Benny and with ventriloquist Edgar Bergen and his dummy, Charlie McCarthy, for thrills with *Spy at Large,* or for crime fighters like the *Green Hornet* and *The Shadow. Lux Radio Theatre* brought adaptations of Broadway shows and Hollywood movies right into people's homes.

Radio linked people in a new way. No longer dependent on newspaper deliveries, news traveled thousands of miles with a single transmission. And everyone could enjoy the same entertainment; laughing, crying, and cheering to the same shows. Radio changed forever the way the world communicates.

Glossary

Allies: during World War II, the nations that joined together to fight against the Nazis, including Great Britain, France, the Soviet Union, and the United States

Axis: the nations, primarily Germany, Italy, and Japan, fighting against the Allies during World War II

Big Band: a group of musicians, including sections of rhythm, brass, and reeds, playing arrangements of jazz and popular music

Charles Lindbergh and the Spirit of St. Louis: Charles Augustus Lindbergh (1902-1974) was an American aviator who made the first solo nonstop flight across the Atlantic from New York to Paris in his plane, the *Spirit of St. Louis.* He completed the journey in 33½ hours on May 20–21, 1927.

Great Depression: the period of great economic hardship in the United States that began with the failure of many banks due to the crash of the Stock Market in 1929, and continued through most of the 1930's

Nazis: Founded in 1919, and abolished in 1945 with the end of WW II, this political party gained control of Germany under the direction of Adolf Hitler in 1933. The Nazis carried out a ruthless program of anti-Semitism, racism, nationalism, and aggression.

Pearl Harbor: On December 7, 1941, the Japanese launched a surprise aerial attack on the United States naval base at Pearl Harbor on Oahu Island, Hawaii, and prompted the United States entry into World War II.

ration coupons: coupons given to families during World War II to turn in when buying items in short supply, such as meat, gasoline, sugar and butter. This insured that these scarce goods were distributed evenly.

World War II: a conflict between the Allies and the Axis powers which is generally considered to have begun in 1939 and concluded in 1945

DATE DUE
